I0012415

JAVASCRIPT FUN AND GAMES: INTERACTIVE ACTIVITIES FOR WEB ENTHUSIASTS

Contents

5

1. 1.1 what is JavaScript exactly?

JavaScript is a crucial tool for creating visually appealing and user-friendly content for games and activities that runs easily in the client's browser. Its ability to control the Record Article Model (DOM) and work with HTML5 features like the Material Programming point of interaction seeks after it a sensible choice for making program based games and activities.

1.2 Why should games and exercises use JavaScript?

Similarity across stages: JavaScript is a cross-stage answer for game improvement since it works with practically all ongoing internet browsers. Customers don't need any additional modules to play around with different gadgets.

Accessibility: As a client-side language, JavaScript grants games and activities to be rapidly open without the prerequisite for foundations or downloads. This receptiveness adds to a reliable client experience.

Utilization of Internet-Based Tools: JavaScript reliably integrates with HTML and CSS, allowing designers to join the power of these advancements to make apparently captivating and wise games and activities.

The growth of the biological system: The JavaScript environment is broad and consistently evolving. For game turn of events, there are a ton of libraries and structures that provide designers with a ton of devices to make the cycle simpler.

1.3 Fundamentals

Before diving into JavaScript for games and activities, it's key to have a fundamental cognizance of:

HTML and CSS: experience with page structure and styling methods. Ideas for Programming: Data on factors, control stream, abilities, and fundamental data structures. Fundamentals of an Internet Browser: comprehending how HTML, CSS, and JavaScript are rendered by internet browsers.

2. Setting Up Your Current circumstance

2.1 Content tools and IDEs

Picking the right content tool or Incorporated Improvement Climate (IDE) is urgent for a smooth improvement experience. The following are popular choices for developing JavaScript:

Code in Visual Studio: A lightweight code editor with a lot of features and great support for JavaScript. It also has syntax highlighting, IntelliSense, and extensions for more features.

Atom: a text editor with a lot of options for customization, a lively community, and a lot of plugins for developing JavaScript.

Stunning Text: Known for its speed and effortlessness, Glorious Text is a flexible manager that upholds JavaScript and offers different bundles for expanding its capacities.

2.2 Browser Developer Tools

Developer tools for profiling and debugging JavaScript code are included in all modern web browsers. Learn about the developer tools that browsers provide, such as:

Chrome by Google: Access Chrome DevTools by right-tapping on a page and choosing "Investigate." Investigate highlights like the Control center, Sources, and Execution tabs.

Mozilla Firefox: Utilize the Firefox Designer Devices by right-clicking and choosing "Investigate Component." The Control center, Debugger, and Organization tabs are especially valuable for JavaScript advancement.

2.3 Rendition Control

Executing adaptation control is fundamental for following changes and working together with others. Platforms like GitHub, GitLab, and Bitbucket offer hosting and collaboration capabilities, and Git is a widely used version control system. Introduce Git on your machine and make a store for your JavaScript game or movement.

slam
Duplicate code
Introduce Git (model for Linux)

```
sudo able get update
sudo able get introduce git
```

3. Nuts and bolts of JavaScript for Games

3.1 Factors and Information Types

JavaScript utilizes factors to store and control information. Understanding information types is pivotal for working with game rationale and client connections.

3.1.1 Factors

Announce factors utilizing let, const, or var:

javascript Copy code with score set to zero;
playerName = "Alice" in const;
var isGameOver = bogus;

3.1.2 Data Types

JavaScript has a variety of data types, including

Types Primitive:

Numbers: let count = 42;
Strings: const welcoming = "Hi";
Booleans: var isPlaying = valid;
Null: let gameResult = invalid;
Undefined: provide highScore;
Complex types:

Arrays: let gameItems = ["sword", "safeguard", "potion"];
Objects:
javascript
Duplicate code
const player = {
 name: " Weave",
 level: 3, the inventory: key", "map"]
};

3.2 Control Stream (if proclamations, circles)

Controlling the progression of your game includes restrictive explanations and circles.

3.2.1 Javascript Copy code with If Statements letting health equal 80;

```javascript
on the off chance that (wellbeing > 0) {
  console.log("Player is alive");
} else {
  console.log("Game over");
```

3.2.2 Loops Copy Javascript code for

```javascript
(let i = 0; i < 5; i++) {
  console.log(i);
}
```

While Circle
javascript
Duplicate code
let commencement = 3;

```
while (commencement > 0) {
 console.log(countdown);
 countdown--;
```

3.3 Functions and Scope

Understanding scope is essential for managing variables. Functions are reusable blocks of code.

3.3.1 Capabilities
javascript
Duplicate code

```
capability greetPlayer(name) {
 console.log("Hello, " + name + "!");
}

greetPlayer("Sam");
```

3.3.2 Scope The javascript Copy code function calculateTotal(score)

```
let bonus equal 10;
 return score + reward;
```

Let totalScore be equal to calculateTotal(50);

```javascript
console.log(totalScore);//   Output: 60
console.log(bonus);// Error: bonus
```

is not specified. 3.4 Arrays and Objects The management of game data relies heavily on arrays and objects.

3.4.1 Exhibits

javascript

Duplicate code

```javascript
let gameLevels = [1, 2, 3, 4];
console.log(gameLevels[2]);//
```

Output: 3 3.4.2 Javascript objects Copy code let player = name: Eve", wellbeing: a total of 100, inventory: shield," "sword");

```javascript
console.log(name  of  player);  //
```

Output: Eve

Understanding these nuts and bolts establishes the groundwork for making game rationale and overseeing information in JavaScript. In the following segment, we'll investigate how to control the Record Item Model (DOM) to make intelligent games.

4. The Report Item Model (DOM) addresses the construction of a page as a tree of articles.

This section of DOM Control

4.1 is the introduction to the Report Article Model (DOM). JavaScript associates with the DOM to invigorate content and answer client exercises logically.

4.1.1 Accessing DOM Components javascript Duplicate code // Selecting components based on ID

```
const header = document.getElementById("header");
```

```
// Picking components in light of their group name const buttons = document.getElementsByClassName("button");
```

```
// Selecting components based on the name of the label const sections = document.getElementsByTagName("p");
```

4.1.2 Changing DOM Components Javascript Duplicate Code

```
// Changing the content of the text
header.textContent = "New Header";
```

```
// Changing the substance of the HTML
paragraphs[0].innerHTML = "Refreshed section content";
```

```
// Changing the CSS styles so that
header.style.color = "blue";
```

4.2 Event Dealing with

Astute games regularly rely upon client exercises. JavaScript is fit for answering client started occasions.

4.2.1 Members of the Event Audience javascript Duplicate code

```
// Adding a tick to the Event Audience
button.addEventListener("click,"
capability()        console.log("Button clicked!");
});
```

4.2.2 Event Thing

javascript

Copy code

```
// Getting to event properties
});
```

with DOM control and occasion management. In the following section, we will examine the Canvas API, which is particularly useful for creating 2D graphics and games.

5. Material Programming connection point for 2D Delineations

5.1 Preamble to the Material Part

The Material Programming point of interaction gives areas of strength for a versatile technique for drawing representations on the web. It's especially useful for intuitive perceptions and 2D games.

5.1.2 Acquiring the 2D Delivering Setting

javascript Duplicate code const material = document.getElementById("gameCanvas"); 5.1.1 Creating a Material HTML Duplicate code

const ctx = canvas.getContext("2d");

5.2.1 Drawing Square Shapes with Javascript Duplicate the code //

Draw a filled square shape with
ctx.fillStyle = "blue;"
ctx.lineWidth = 2;
strokeRect(200, 50, 80, and 120) in
ctx

5.2.2 Drawing Circles

javascript
Copy code

```
// Draw a filled circle
ctx.beginPath();
ctx.arc(400, 150, 30, 0, 2 PI);
ctx.fillStyle = "green";
ctx.fill();
```

```
// Draw a stroked circle
ctx.beginPath();
Math. ctx.arc(550, 150, 40, 0),
strokeStyle in ctx = "purple";
ctx.lineWidth = 3;
ctx.stroke();
```

5.2.3 Drawing Ways

javascript

```
Copy code
// Draw a custom way
ctx.beginPath();
change to (100, 300); lineTo(200,
400); ctx
lineFrom(300, 350); ctx.closePath()
in ctx
ctx.fillStyle = "orange";
ctx.fill();
```

5.3 Movement Basics

5.3.1   Requesting   Movement
Packaging
javascript
Copy code
capacity vivify() {

```
requestAnimationFrame(animate);
 // Utilize energize() to do the
liveliness rationale.
```

5.3.2 Dismantling the Canvas by utilizing the javascript Copy code function clearCanvas() and

```
ctx.clearRect(0,    0,    canvas.width,
canvas.height);
requestAnimationFrame(animate)
```
utilizing the capability enliven()
```
 clearCanvas();
 // Perform vivacity reasoning here
}
```

5.3.3 Reviving and Conveying Game Things

javascript
Copy code
```
class Player {
  constructor(x, y, clear) {
   this.x = x;
   this.y = y;
   sweep; this.radius =
  }

  draw() {
   ctx.beginPath();
   ctx.arc(this.x, this.y, this.radius, 0,
2*Mathematics PI);
```

```
    fillStyle = "blue" in ctx;
    ctx.fill();
  update()//Execute player update
rationale in this area. const player =
new Player(100, 100, 20,)

capacity stimulate() {

requestAnimationFrame(animate);
  clearCanvas();
  player.update();
  player.draw();
}

vitalize();
```

The Material Programming point of interaction opens up open doors for making obviously captivating and instinctive 2D games. The specifics of creating intelligent games with JavaScript, such as game circles, client input handling, and impact discovery, will be discussed in the following section.

6. Making Intelligent Games

6.1 Game Circle

A game circle is essential for delivering and refreshing game components constantly. It ensures smooth and consistent intuitiveness.

6.1.1 Javascript's Duplicate Code Capability for Game Circle Design

```
gameLoop()
requestAnimationFrame(gameLoop
);
 modify(); // GameLoop renders
game elements;// Game rationale
render() is updated.
```

6.2 Managing Client Data

Getting and noting client input is fundamental for making astute games.

6.2.2 The javascript code for the mouse input is as follows: 6.2.1 Keyboard input javascript Copy code

```
document.addEventListener("keydown", function(event) if (event.key === "ArrowUp") // Handle the up arrow key else if (event.key === "ArrowDown") // Add more key handling as needed const mouseX = event.clientX - canvas.getBoundingClientRect().left canvas.addEventListener("mousemove", function(event))
  const Dreary = event.clientY - canvas.getBoundingClientRect().top;
  // Handle mouse improvement
});

canvas.addEventListener("click," function(event)) = const mouseX -
```

canvas.getBoundingClientRect().left
;
 const   Drab   =
canvas.getBoundingClientRect().top
+ event.clientY;

 // Control mouse click 6.3 Collision Detection Collision detection is essential for determining when game objects interact.

6.3.1 Hopping Box Crash

javascript
Copy code

```javascript
capacity     detectCollision(object1, object2) {
 return (
   object1.x    <    object2.x    + object2.width &&
   object1.x    +    object1.width    > object2.x &&
```

```
object1.y < object2.y +
object2.height &&
```

6.4 Game Over and Scorekeeping Conditions

Implementing game over and scorekeeping conditions enhances your game's depth.

6.4.1 Scorekeeping
javascript
Copy code
```
let score = 0;

capability increaseScore(points)
where score approaches focuses;
```
6.4.2 Game Over Duplicate code
```
capability checkGameOver() if
(playerHealth = 0) gameOver();
 }
}
```

```
ability gameOver() {
  // Perform game over exercises
  console.log("Game Over!");
}
```

7. Significant level Subjects

7.1 WebSockets for Multiplayer Games

Making multiplayer games incorporates consistent correspondence between players. WebSockets give a bidirectional correspondence channel.

7.1.1 Using Javascript to Setup a WebSocket Duplicate Code // Client-side const attachment = new WebSocket("ws://your-server-address");

```
 console.log("WebSocket affiliation
spread out");
});
```

```
information =
JSON.parse(event.data);
```

```
socket.addEventListener("message,
" function(event));
 // Handle messages that come in);

// WebSocket = require("ws") on
the server (Node.js model);
new WebSocket = const server Port
(server): 3000 });

server.on("connection",
function(socket)),                and
console.log("WebSocket connection
established")

 // Impress the client with your
message
socket.send(JSON.stringify(type:    "
message's content: Welcome to the
game!" }));
});
```

7.2 WebGL for 3D Plans

WebGL considers hardware accelerated 3D plans in the program.

7.2.1 Making a WebGL Setting javascript Duplicate the accompanying code: const material =

```
document.getElementById("webglCanvas")
const gl = canvas.getContext("webgl");

if (! gl) {
 console.error("Unable to present WebGL. Your program may not help it.");
}
```

7.2.2 Drawing 3D Articles

javascript

Copy code

```
// Describe vertex and part shaders
```

```
const vertexShaderSource = '
 quality vec4 aVertexPosition;
 uniform mat4 uModelViewMatrix;
 mat4 uniform; uProjectionMatrix

  gl_Position = uProjectionMatrix *
uModelViewMatrix                *
aVertexPosition;
 }
`;

const fragmentShaderSource = '
 }
`;

// Assemble shaders, make a
program, and association it
// Set up pads, properties, and
formal attire
// Draw 3D things
// (Bare essential WebGL plan goes
past the degree of this model)
```

7.3 Sound and Video Blend

Further develop the gaming experience by combining sound and video parts.

7.3.1 Sound
javascript
Copy code

```
const sound = new Audio("path/to/sound.mp3");

ability playSound() {
  audio.play();
}
```

7.3.2 Video
html
Copy code

 Your program doesn't maintain the video tag.

To further develop your game advancement capacities, investigate the abilities of WebSockets, WebGL, and media components. In the accompanying region, we'll discuss propelling execution and watching out for typical challenges in game new development.

8. Building Explicit Games and Exercises

8.1 Making a Basic Test Game

8.1.1 Game Construction

Show questions and different decision responds to.

Track the player's score.

Give criticism on right and mistaken replies.

Show the last score toward the end.

8.1.2 Execution

Characterize a variety of items, each addressing an inquiry with choices and the right response.

Use DOM control to progressively show questions and choices.

Execute occasion audience members for client choice and score following.

8.2 Structure a Memory Matching Game

8.2.1 Game Design

Show a matrix of face-down cards.

Permit the player to flip two cards all at once.

Check for matches and update the score.

End the game when all matches are coordinated.

8.2.2 Execution

Make an exhibit with sets of card pictures.

Randomize the order of the cards by shuffle the array.

Utilize the Material Programming interface or DOM control to make the game board.

Execute occasion audience members for card snaps and game rationale.

8.3 Planning a Platformer Game

8.3.1 Game Construction

Make a person that can move left, right, and hop.

Plan stages and obstructions.

Make use of collision detection and gravity.

Add adversaries and enhancers.

8.3.2 Execution

Utilize the Material Programming interface for delivering the game world.

Execute a game circle for consistent updates.

Handle client input for character development.

Identify impacts with stages, obstructions, and adversaries.

Incorporate sound for a more vivid encounter.

8.4 Fostering a Riddle Game

8.4.1 Game Construction

Show a framework based puzzle.

Permit the player to move pieces to settle the riddle.

Track the quantity of moves or time taken to finish the riddle.

The puzzle board can be constructed using either HTML elements or the Canvas API.

Execute simplified usefulness for moving pieces.

Track user actions by incorporating event listeners.

Give criticism when the riddle is effectively tackled.

These particular game models cover a scope of types and show how to apply the major ideas of JavaScript game turn of events. Go ahead and alter and develop these plans to make your own remarkable games and exercises. We will investigate mobile responsiveness and game layout adaptations for various devices in the following section.

9. Versatile Responsiveness

9.1 Touch Occasions and Versatile Info

9.1.1 Touch Occasions

javascript

Duplicate code

```
  const            Tricky            =
event.touches[0].clientY            -
canvas.getBoundingClientRect().top
;
  // Touch start with the handle;



  // Handle contact end
});
```

9.2 Adjusting Game Designs for Various Gadgets

9.2.1 Responsive Plan Standards

Utilize relative units (rates, viewport units) for estimating components.

Media inquiries can change styles in view of screen size and direction.
Test your game on various gadgets to guarantee a steady encounter.

9.2.2 Viewport Meta Tag

html

Duplicate code

```
<!-- Incorporate the viewport meta label in the top of your HTML document - - >
<meta name="viewport" content="width=device-width, starting scale=1.0">
```

9.2.3 CSS Media Inquiries

css

Duplicate code

```
/* Characterize styles for little screens */
@media just screen and (max-width: 600px) /* Define styles for medium screens / @media only screen and /* Adjust styles for small
```

screens 601px) and the maximum width: 1024px) {

 /* Change styles for medium screens */

}

/* Characterize styles for huge screens */

@media just screen and (min-width: 1025px) /* Adjust styles for large screens //

9.3 Testing on Mobile Devices

 9.3.1 Browser Developer Tools Emulate various devices and test responsiveness with browser developer tools.

9.3.2 Remote Debugging Make use of browser-based remote debugging tools by connecting your mobile device to your development machine.

javascript Copy code // Chrome example // 1. Open Chrome on your work area with remote troubleshooting empowered.

// 2. Associate your cell phone to a similar organization.

// 3. Open Chrome on your cell phone and explore to chrome://assess.

// 4. Track down your gadget and investigate your game.

9.3.3 Cross-Program Similarity

Test your game on various portable programs (Chrome, Safari, Firefox) to guarantee similarity.

Guaranteeing versatile responsiveness is fundamental for contacting a more extensive crowd. By integrating contact occasions, responsive plan standards, and intensive testing, you can improve your game for a consistent encounter on different gadgets.

Techniques for testing and debugging your game will be discussed in the final section.

10. Testing and Investigating

10.1 Utilizing Program Engineer Instruments

10.1.1 Control center Logging
javascript
Duplicate code
console.log("Debugging data");
10.1.2 Breakpoints Using breakpoints, you can halt the execution of your code and examine variables.
10.1.3 Investigating Components
Utilize the "Components" tab to review and change HTML and CSS progressively.
10.1.4 Network Tab Keep an eye on network requests to find errors or bottlenecks in performance.
10.1.5 Execution Tab
Examine execution to recognize regions for enhancement.

10.2 Unit Testing for Games

10.2.1 Testing Game Rationale

Compose unit tests for basic game rationale capabilities.

Use testing structures like Jasmine, Mocha, or Quip.

javascript

Duplicate code

```javascript
// Model utilizing Joke
test("Addition capability adds two numbers accurately", () => {
  expect(add(2, 3)).toBe(5);
});
```

10.3 Troubleshooting Procedures

10.3.1 Chrome DevTools

Influence Chrome DevTools for top to bottom investigating:

Set breakpoints.

Step through code.

Investigate factors.

Screen network movement.

10.3.2 Cross-Program Testing

Test your game on various programs (Chrome, Firefox, Safari) to guarantee similarity.

10.3.3 Versatile Testing

Test your game on different cell phones to guarantee a smooth versatile encounter.

10.3.4 Mistake Taking care of

Execute strong blunder dealing with to deal with unforeseen circumstances nimbly.

javascript Copy code, try, // Risky code, catch (error), console.error("An error occurred:"), and catch (error). error.message);

10.4 Boosting Performance

10.4.1 Reducing File Size Minify and bundle your JavaScript files.

10.4.2 Picture Pressure

Pack pictures to limit stacking times.

10.4.3 Code Parting

Part your code into more modest pieces and burden them on request.

10.4.4 Reserving

Carry out storing techniques to lessen server demands.

10.5 Cross-Program Similarity

10.5.1 Prefixing CSS

Use merchant prefixes to guarantee similarity with various programs.

css

Duplicate code

```css
.model {
  -webkit-change: change (50%, 50%)
  transform: change (50%, 50%)
}
```

10.5.2 Polyfills

Incorporate polyfills for missing elements in more established programs.

html

Duplicate code

```
<script
src="https://cdn.polyfill.io/v3/polyfill.min.js"></script>
```

Testing and troubleshooting are basic stages in game turn of events. By utilizing program engineer instruments, composing unit tests, and improving execution, you can guarantee your game capabilities well across different stages and programs. This finishes up the aide on JavaScript for games and exercises. Best of luck with your game advancement attempts!

11.Static Website Hosting

Platforms Like GitHub Pages, Netlify, and Vercel Provide Simple Deployment Options for Static Websites

11.1.2 Cloud Services For scalability and performance,

put your game on cloud platforms like AWS, Google Cloud, or Azure.

11.1.3 Game Development Platforms For sharing and distributing your game, investigate game-specific platforms like Game Jolt or itch.io.

11.2.1 Minification and Compression To speed up the loading times of your JavaScript, CSS, and HTML files, compress them.

11.2.2 Picture Improvement

Improve and pack pictures to diminish record sizes without forfeiting quality.

11.2.3 Code Parting

Execute code parting to stack just the essential code for each page or element.

11.3 Cross-Program Similarity

11.3.1 Program Testing

Test your game on various programs (Chrome, Firefox, Safari) to guarantee similarity.

11.3.2 Versatile Responsiveness

Check that your game capabilities well on different cell phones and screen sizes.

11.4 Area and SSL

11.4.1 Area Enlistment

Register a custom space to upgrade the impressive skill of your game's URL.

11.4.2 SSL Certificate Obtain and configure an SSL certificate for HTTPS to protect your game.

11.5 Consistent Arrangement

11.5.1 Mechanized Arrangement
Set up consistent combination and constant sending (CI/Compact disc) pipelines for robotized organization.

11.5.2 Git Snares
Use Git snares to set off sending scripts while pushing changes to your store.

11.6 Checking and Investigation

11.6.1 Blunder Following
Carry out mistake following devices to recognize and fix issues continuously.

11.6.2 Examination
Incorporate investigation apparatuses to accumulate bits of knowledge into client conduct and

further develop the client experience.

11.7 Last Agenda

Twofold actually look at all resources, contents, and conditions are accurately connected.

Check that your game's usefulness stays in one piece after sending.

Examine user interactions, high scores, and any features that are server-dependent.

11.8 Maintenance after the deployment

Keep an eye on the server's performance and scale resources as necessary.

Respond promptly to user-reported issues.

Consider delivering refreshes or new highlights to keep your game locking in.

Congratulations! The time has come to deploy your game. By keeping these organization rules, you guarantee a smooth and expert experience for players getting to your game on the web. Best of luck with the delivery!

End

Congrats on finishing the JavaScript for Games and Exercises guide! You now have the fundamental knowledge and practical skills to create engaging and interactive web-based games thanks to this journey. How about we recap the key focal points:

Basics of JavaScript: Know what variables, data types, control flow, functions, arrays, and objects are all about.

DOM Control: Figure out how to powerfully refresh HTML and CSS through the Report Item Model (DOM) utilizing JavaScript.

Material Programming interface for 2D Illustrations: Explore the Canvas API to create games with appealing visuals by drawing shapes, paths, and animations.

Development of Interactive Games: Jump into game advancement ideas, including the game circle, client input taking care of, crash identification, scorekeeping, and game over conditions.

High level Subjects: Investigate more advanced topics like the integration of audio and video, WebGL for 3D graphics, and WebSockets for multiplayer games.

Constructing Particular Games and Activities: Acquire involved insight by building explicit games, for example, tests, memory matching games, platformers, and riddles.

Mobile-Friendly Design: Figure out how to adjust game designs for various gadgets and carry out touch occasions for versatile info.

Testing and Investigating: Ace testing strategies, troubleshooting with program engineer apparatuses, unit testing, and improving execution.

Deployment: Learn about continuous deployment, cross-browser compatibility, and deployment strategies optimized for production.

Conclusion: You will have a comprehensive understanding of game development with JavaScript at the end of your journey, from the fundamentals to advanced topics and deployment.

www.ingramcontent.com/pod-product-compliance
Lightning Source LLC
LaVergne TN
LVHW051616050326
832903LV00033B/4529